SECRET FINANCIAL ANALYSIS AND MODELLING FOR BEGINNERS!

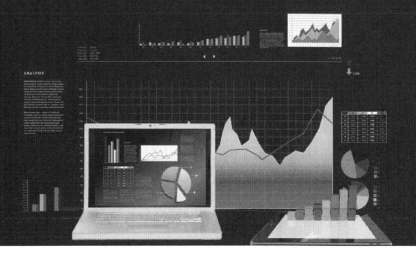

TABLE OF CONTENTS

LEGAL NOTES AND DISCLAIMER

Text Copyright © [Andrei Besedin]

INTRODUCTION

Henry Ford once said, "Before Everything Else, Getting Ready is the Secret of Financial Success."

Financial success is not easy to achieve and requires adherence to certain basic principles and financial discipline.

It is not the property of a privileged few but can be achieved by anyone who works hard for it and resorts to financial planning. Yes, even you can become rich and have a strong financial position if you are willing to work for it. Accept it and make a commitment that you will achieve it.

The process of achieving financial success is a continuous one and involves setting goals and working to achieve them, while making corrections and modifications as we proceed forward.

The one thing, however, that we need to remember is that different people perceive financial success in different ways. While some believe that achieving financial success is to have adequate monetary resources to take care of their lives even after retirement, there are others who wish to have all the luxuries of life, besides a hefty bank balance and assets for the benefit of their family and children. Again, there are some people who are satisfied with a position in which they have no debt and are earning a reasonably good amount of money to take care of their regular expenses.

Different perceptions about financial success point to the development of unique and customised financial plans for each individual and organization. But everyone wants to have adequate funds and have more choices in life. The this article will talk about the eight basic steps that are crucial to financial planning and can help Australians become financially disciplined and achieve financial success.

Set a life goal plan

Goal setting is a powerful process of thinking about your ideal future and for motivating yourself to turn your vision of a perfect life into reality. It is a key step in attaining success, especially financial success. This requires the identification of what you aim to achieve and in what time frame. Think of where you would like to be in two, five, ten or twenty years from today. Identify what you wish to achieve and be clear about your personal goals. Make a note of your goals: whether you want to fund your children's tertiary education, purchase an new house, go for a holiday every year or plan for retirement.

The next step is to set a time frame with which you wish to achieve these goals. It is crucial that you be specific and set a clear date. If done properly, your goals will range from short, medium to long term. Visualise what you will be thinking and feeling when that date arrives and you have successfully achieved your goal.

Finally, identify the quantum of funds, you need for each of your goals and then set a total figure accordingly. This should be done keeping in mind the rising inflation levels. You also need to chalk out a strategy (or strategies) that outline where you are currently and where you would like to reach.

Spend less than you earn

Excessive spending is a major reason why people face financial difficulties. So it is vital for you to implement a system that involves identifying your sources of income as well as the expenses. This step also involves an analysis of all your expenses and identification of the expenses that can be reduced or done away with entirely to boost your overall savings level.

Nobody can achieve financial success by spending more than what they earn. Savings play an important role in helping you achieve your financial goals. So, your aim should be to maximize savings. An analysis of your expenses will reveal that a little cost cutting on various fronts can result in significant savings.

Your Biggest Asset, Don't Risk It

There is an old saying in the life insurance industry that life insurance is not bought, it's sold. Not surprisingly, it's not until you sit in front of a professional advisor that you begin to appreciate what you and your family stand to lose if the unthinkable occurs.

Personal life insurance policies have been compared to an umbrella salesman who is always willing to sell you an umbrella until it starts raining. Therefore it is recommended that this important area of your financial affairs is addressed early and completely.

The important questions to ask when implementing your personal insurance policies are:

How much is enough?

How should the premiums be structured?

Who should pay for the insurance premiums?

Who should you insure with?

Focus on Reducing Tax

Taxes may take away a large part of your income. An important step in financial planning is look for ways to reduce your tax payments. A proactive tax strategy will allow you take advantage of the various tax breaks provided by the government and benefit from various incentives available on investments in certain areas. You can reduce your tax liability by:

Making contributions to your superannuation fund.

Prepaying interest is a common strategy used to claim interest deductions on your margin loans or investment property loan. You can claim a tax deduction on interest payments as long as the loan is used to generate taxable income. In case of margin loans, the interest rate is likely to be reduced when you make your payments in advance.

You can offset capital gains tax by claiming losses incurred on the sale of some other asset.

If possible, defer some of your income to the next year because tax is payable on income when you actually receive it,

Claim for a tax rebate on medical and other allowable expenses.

You can also take the advice of a financial expert on further ways to reduce your tax liability.

Lose that 'Bad Debt,' reduce that 'Good Debt' and manage that 'Smart Debt.'

'Bad' debt is borrowing money, typically at high interest rates, to buy something destined to go down in value. Usually this debt provides no tax advantage.

Using 'easy finance' or a credit card to buy a wide screen TV is an example of 'bad debt.' Paying well over 10% interest on a personal loan from the bank to buy a second hand car is another example of bad debt. In both of these cases, you're not really buying a asset as both the TV and the car will be worth considerably less than they initially cost long before the loan is paid out.

The characteristics of 'bad' debt are high interest, no tax advantages and the purchase of something set to go down in value over time. Borrowing money to pay for holiday is arguably even worse than bad debt as you are left with nothing except few happy snap to show for it.

For most of us, 'good' debt is the unpaid mortgage on the property we live in. Whilst the interest repayments are not tax deductible, your home will at least grow in value in the long term. And, you get somewhere to live without paying rent. The characteristics of 'good debt' are a low interest rate and the potential for the asset to grow in value.

So, if the upside of 'bad' debt is 'good debt,' what is the upside of 'good' debt? It's called 'smart' and is defined as debt: That has an low interest rate is used to purchase an asset that grows in value that purchases an income producing asset, hence the interest costs maybe tax deductible.

Get an Investment Portfolio

We all have different ideas about what level of risk we are comfortable with. Some of us love the rush of adrenaline we get from skydiving, while others find simply diving into a pool to be plenty of excitement. It's partly to do with where we are in life and partly, it's just a personality thing. Some people hear the word 'risk' and think 'danger'; others hear the word 'risk' and think 'woo hoo!'

One thing investors ⬜uickly learn is that you cannot control investment markets. Volatility is part of investing. What you can control is your investment strategy - having the framework in place to give you the best chance of meeting your goals and expectations and aligning investments to your risk profile.

Taking some time to plan your strategy before you start investing can be the difference between achieving your goals and simply aspiring to them.

Having a clear idea of your investment objectives, timeframe, and attitude to risk provides a solid basis on which to build your investment portfolio. The more specific you are, the better your chances of success.

Just like life, your investment plan is a work in progress. It should be flexible enough to cater for changes and market challenges - both big and small.

Can the Government Help?

Governments play an important role in providing a safety net from which we are all protected. In Australia, Centrelink is the statutory authority responsible for delivering services on behalf of the Department of Families, Housing, Community Services & Indigenous Affairs and the Department of Education, Employment and Workplace Relations.

Unfortunately, many people just do not realize they are entitled to assistance or payments from the government. An example that illustrates this point can be found in early 2011 when the Australian Minister for Child Care released a report estimating that up to 100,000 Australian families, thought to be eligible for the Child Care Benefit or Child Care Rebate payments were not claiming that entitlement.

It is never too early to familiarize with the benefits Centre link administers and seek information on how these benefits can be claimed.

Where there's a will, there's a way

Making financial and legal arrangements about the transfer of your personal assets to chosen beneficiaries can be difficult and emotional. An integral part of the financial planning process is ensuring that the assets which are accumulated during a person's lifetime are disposed of of in accordance with their wishes upon death.

Approximately 50% of Australians die without having a current Will. Many people would not be too concerned about this statistic as they believe their assets will automatically pass to their spouse or family on death.

An integral part of the financial planning process is ensuring that the assets which are accumulated during a person's lifetime are disposed of by their wishes upon death.

IMPORTANCE OF SPREADSHEETS

Spreadsheets are integral part of the 21st century economy. Most businesses today rely on spreadsheets in a some way. The multi-celled document is used heavily for corporate and transactional intelligence; spreadsheets are used for a variety of reasons which cover all aspect of accounting and mathematics. They include budgeting, charting/graphing, financial analysis, and scientific applications. Spreadsheet programs also assist in managing data in different formats.

Spreadsheets in the News

Spreadsheet errors can happen to the best of us. Spreadsheet typos and oversights can wind up costing your company millions. Financial regulations, such as Sarbanes-Oxley re□uirements, have had a huge impact on how companies manage changes and controls in financial documents, such as spreadsheets. Because of their preponderance and the amount of digital fingertips that can touch these documents, spreadsheets have come under a lot of fire. In particular, companies lack the appropriate controls and repeatable processes to mitigate the risks.

Research abounds on the prominence of spreadsheet errors. Research has repeatedly shown that an alarming proportion of corporate spreadsheet models are not tested to the extent necessary to support directors' fiduciary, reporting and compliance obligations. This isn't about software defects within the applications, such as Microsoft Excel, Google Spreadsheets or OpenOffice. The problems associated with a spreadsheet ordinarily do not reside in the software program itself. It's those imperfect human beings who are using the applications: inputting data, copying and pasting numbers from row to row and column to column, and writing inaccurate formulae.

Risk of Spreadsheets

Spreadsheets enable us □uickly to perform analysis that would otherwise be difficult or time-consuming to prepare. We all use them because we love the flexibility that comes with them. The problem is that we tend to place undue trust in the integrity of the analysis that we prepare. Errors happen. Given tight deadlines and pressures of work, errors arise more often than we would like. The simplest of errors, often arising as a result of a copy and paste error, a misplaced insert row or a poor assumption, can have catastrophic effects.

Lack of Spreadsheet controls and security and integrity issues create colossal challenges. These risks include: lost revenue and profits; wrong pricing and poor decision-making due to prevalent but undetected errors; fraud due to malicious tampering; and difficulties in demonstrating fiduciary and regulatory compliance.

There are extensive research base on the risks of using spreadsheets within business. The main known risks of spreadsheets include:

Human Error - To err is human, hence the majority of spreadsheets contain errors. Because spreadsheets are rarely tested these errors remain. Recent research has shown that spreadsheet models used operationally have material defects.

Fraud - Because of the ease with which program code and data are mixed, spreadsheets are the perfect environment for perpetrating fraud.

Overconfidence - Because spreadsheet users do not go looking for errors, they don't find any or many. Spreadsheet users are therefore overconfident in their use of spreadsheets.

Interpretation - Translation of a business problem into the spreadsheet domain can lead to a position where decision makers may act in the belief that decisions can be made with confidence on the output from the spreadsheet despite evidence to the contrary.

Archiving - Poor archiving can lead to weaknesses in spreadsheet control that contribute to operational risk.

It has been suggested that there may be a further series of systemic risks posed by spreadsheets including (but not limited to!) Assumptions, Opacity, Reification and Enterprise Interoperability.

To minimize risks while gaining the inherent BI value of spreadsheets, information and knowledge management professionals must discriminate between the different ways spreadsheets are used. Then, they must help users apply advanced spreadsheet tools and techniques to their daily jobs, while also implementing a tightly controlled (or closely monitored) environment for critical production processes that rely on spreadsheet data.

Spreadsheets Controls

Spreadsheet Profiling is the first step of the process of analyzing data to determine its structure and meaning. Various processes are performed to reveal patterns, Metadata matches, value completeness, and so on. Spreadsheet Profiling is emerging as an important requirement for business users to gain full value from spreadsheet assets.

A picture is worth a thousand words... A spreadsheet formula [= 1 + 1] in a cell return an output of [33.00]. Here is a simple spreadsheet example providing a convenient manufactured but incorrect output and no errors or warnings are generated for the spreadsheet user.

Could this happen to one of your key spreadsheets - intentionally or unintentionally and how your decisions may be influenced?

SECRETS OF BUSINESS SUCCESS

Over half of all new businesses fail in the first five years. Only one in ten will last ten years. Know the odds and plan to beat them with basic, tried and true business sense; starting with:

- ☐ Motivation and stamina

- ☐ Good research and planning

- ☐ Good choice of business (fill a need)

- ☐ Good location

Good management

- ☐ Good marketing strategy

- ☐ Good financing

- ☐ Good employees

Know the Laws

When planning your business, be sure to find out about applicable zoning for the location you are considering, necessary business licenses, insurance, etc.

If you have employees in your business, it is important to be knowledgeable about employment laws relating to work hours, minimum wage, workers' safety e☐ual opportunities, workers' compensation and required insurance for workers.

Hidden Costs

If you work for yourself, you will be re☐uired to pay your own Social Security tax and federal and state withholding on a quarterly basis. You will also need to cover the cost of our health insurance and retirement benefits. If you have employees, you will have to cover these costs for them also.

Consult with a lawyer, accountant or other business professional about tax re☐uirements, and employment laws.

Finding the Money

Every entrepreneur needs money to get started. Funds may come from your own savings, the resources of friends, family or investors. A common place to secure financing is from a bank. Before going to a bank or other financing sources, it is important that you organize some information about your business so that you will be prepared to answer ☐uestions, be clear about your goals and financial needs, and you will be more successful at securing a loan.

Business Structures

There are several types of business structures to consider before starting your own business. These include:

1) Sole proprietorship

2) Partnership

3) Corporation

4) limited Liability Corporation

5) Non-profit corporation and

6) Cooperative.

Each structure has advantages and disadvantages regarding decision-making, profit-sharing, and taxation. It is a good idea to research each structure and then talk to an accountant, a lawyer or other business professional before deciding on which structure will work best for your business.

The Business Plan

A business plan includes the following information:

☐ Name of Business

☐ Name of Owner(s)

☐ Location and Phone Number of Business

☐ Definition of your Business (1-2 sentences)

☐ What you are offering (selling)

☐ What your goals are

☐ What makes it unique or better

☐ Financial Analysis

☐ Start-up costs; rent, advertising, inventory, equipment, utilities, etc.

☐ Estimated sales, expenses, profits

☐ One-year budget

☐ Marketing Analysis

- Definition of your market

- Evaluation of your competition

- Price structure for your services or goods

- An advertising plan

- A plan for selling or distributing your goods or services

This information should be organized in a clear way. The library has several texts which will help you develop your business plan. Several top-rated software packages also will help you write your business plan including website comprehensive templates.

In addition to your business plan, gather the following information:

- Sources of Collateral - personal assets that you have which you can offer as security for a loan (real estate, investments, cash, personal property, etc.). A bank will almost certainly require collateral.

- Down Payment - cash that you are providing for your business start-up. Banks will expect you to make a personal financial investment in your business.

- Credit Record - documentation of all participating owners' personal net worth.

- Management Ability - show resumes or outlines of job-related experience and education of all managers.

- Ability to repay the loan - cash flow projections including monthly loan payments from the budget in your business plan.

Organize all your information in a clear way. Make two copies - one for you and one for the loan officer. Make an appointment ahead of time. Answer all questions honestly and directly. If one bank turns you down, try another. Organization, thoroughness and planning are important to running your business and in getting a loan.

9 SECRETS TO MAKING LASER-ACCURATE FINANCIALDECISIONS FOR BEGINNERS

Making top notch financial decisions is the goal of all good managers. Unlock these secrets to make a start on this process today.

- Think Widely on Options to Solve the Problem

It is a waste of your time if you make decisions without canvassing ALL the options. How can the business be served well if you haven't bothered to think of all the ways to solve your financial problem?

For example, if you are required to find a replacement for an aging computer system or factory plant item, what options would you think were available? What questions would you ask?

- Replace with a comparable item?

- Repair, upgrade, refurbish or maintain the current item?

- Purchase new/second-hand item with more capacity and increased output?

- Will the customers still be there for the outputs of the new equipment over its life?

- Will the company's direction still provide a need for this asset over its life?

- What are competitors likely to be doing during the life of the asset?

- Will the cost of the new equipment price the product out of the market?

☐ Think Outside the Box

Now that you have thought of good questions it's time to apply some creative thinking processes to them in order to get the best answers.

There are many tools for creative thinking available. Just go to your favorite search engine and type in "creative thinking" for a host of suggestions. Some commonly used ones are:

- Brainstorming

- Plus Minus Interesting (PMI)

- "Six Thinking Hats"

- S.C.A.M.P.E.R.

- Lateral Thinking

- Random Input

Enter any of these into the search engine for an explanation of the terms.

Also you can also gain some real insights by listening to dissenters in your company or other outsiders. They may just have the key that will make your decisions a lot easier and generate more profits for the company. Do not forget to include their ideas.

These tools are designed to provide you with many answers to your questions

☐ *Gather ALL the Data,*

To make a successful financial decision you will need as much data as you can use effectively. You will need to quantify the costs and benefits so that a rational decision can be made easily. The best way to do this is to convert them all to dollars. This will make it easier to assess competing options.

Some Costs to Consider:

- Installation of new equipment

- Removal of current equipment

- Downtime costs e.g. lost orders, increased stocking costs, extra labor to catch up with customer orders

- Training costs for new equipment

- New maintenance costs

- Capital costs

- Tendering costs, purchasing costs

- Initial transport costs

Some Benefits to Consider:

- Less wastage

- Less labor input

- Less resource inputs

- Increased safety

- Increased quality of life

- Faster customer response

- More accurate data

- Faster production times

- Less stock required

- Scrap/Trade-in Value at end of economic life

- Scrap/Trade-in Value of current equipment

Analyze the Data

Now that you have collected the data and have converted it to dollars, it is time to evaluate each viable option using a systematic method.

There is a proven, tested method called Cost Benefit Analysis, which is the tool of choice for these kinds of decisions. It can be used efficiently for asset replacement decisions as well as funding choices. Big business and governments around the world use it. The US government is a big user of this techni☐ue. In fact, it has legislated, federally, that this method be used when making decisions regarding funding to various major programs.

This method allows you to weigh up the relative costs and benefits of competing proposals, showing you which option is the most profitable, least costly or provides the greatest net benefit.

There are certain rules that need to be adhered to so that the final decision can be understood and acted upon. You can find the link to a site offering this proven method at the end of this article or in the Author Profile.

☐ *Make the Decision*

Based on the Cost Benefit Analysis results produced above, there should be a clear answer as to the best way forward - provided all the processes were completed correctly.

You can be confident that this is the best financial decision, given the information at hand and the assumptions underlying the analysis.

☐ *Sell the Decision,*

Once the decision is made it needs to be communicated, since others will need to know. Some groups who may need to know and be convinced that your decision is in their best interests are:

- Employees

- Board members

- The press

- Customers

- Suppliers

- The owners

- Special interest groups

Since you used a tested, proven system to make the decision it makes it easier to convince these groups of the correctness of your decision - saving you time and effort.

Review the Decision

A year after the decision has been made, communicated to stakeholders and implemented it is time to go back and review the decision. This is often referred to as a Post Completion Review. Some areas of review are listed below:

- Assumptions - were they correct?

- Costs - did the actual costs of purchase, installation and operation equal the assumed costs in the proposal?

- Were there other costs involved that were not planned for originally?

- Benefits - did they eventuate? Were they in line with the first assumptions?

- Were there any problems in implementation not foreseen in the proposal?

- Did the decision and implementation involve all the people who could add value?

Learn the Lessons

Once the uestions above have answers there will be lessons that can be learned from the experience. Lessons such as:

- We need to include all of the costs next time - some critical ones was missed

- Some of the benefits did not eventuate - we were not careful enough to think through how these would be created

- Some critical staff members were left out of the decision-making process, but could have assisted to make the process less costly and run more smoothly

- The process of cost benefit analysis has taught us to think more critically about important financial decisions

Apply the Lessons

So that the errors or mistakes in this proposal are not transferred on to the next proposal, the lessons above need to be applied.

Some ways this can occur as follows:

- Hold meetings at the executive level where the Post Completion Reviews and the lessons learned are discussed.

- Use the company newsletter to discuss how future decisions will be conducted based on the lessons learned.

- It makes senior managers accountable for their financial decisions; make part of their salary contingent upon their decision performance.

- Establish a company-wide culture of making good financial decisions using tools that can positively produce the best outcomes.

This is but a short summary of a very expansive topic. It is hoped that this article will provide a springboard for you to begin making better decisions - maybe as early as today.

SECTION1: FINANCIAL RATIOS

CHAPTER 1.

BASIC FINANCIAL STATEMENT ANALYSIS

Financial ratios are a convenient way to summarize large quantities of financial data and to compare firms' performance. They enable investors to take a unique look at the inner workings of companies - but do not substitute for a crystal ball. They won't tell you all of the company's innermost secrets nor will they answer all of your questions. They will, however, give you a firm foundation to build your analysis and subsequent investment decisions.

Before getting started, it is imperative to distinguish between the three most important financial statements:

*Income Statement - a financial statement that shows the revenues, expenses and net income of a firm over a period of time

*Balance Sheet - a financial statement that shows the value of the firm's assets and liabilities at a particular time

*Statement of Cash Flows - a financial statement that tracks cash coming into and flowing out of a firm over a period of time

When it comes to various financial ratios, they can be categorized into four broad groups:

*Leverage Ratios - show how heavily a firm is in debt and measures its ability to meet financial obligations

*Liquidity Ratios - measure how easily a firm can convert its assets into cash

*Efficiency Ratios - measure how productively the firm is using its assets

*Profitability Ratios - measure a firm's return on its investments, giving an overall indication of its performance

Now let's take a look at some of these ratios.

Leverage Ratios

*Long-Term Debt Ratio = long-term debt / long-term debt + equity

*Debt-Equity Ratio = long-term debt / equity

*Total Debt Ratio = total liabilities / total assets

*Times Interest Earned = EBIT / interest payments

*Cash Coverage Ratio = EBIT + depreciation / interest payments

*Fixed-charge Coverage Ratio = EBIT + depreciation / interest payments + (debt repayment)/(1 - tax rate)

Liquidity Ratios

*Net Working Capital to assets = net working capital / total assets

*Current Ratio = current assets / current liabilities

*Quick Ratio = cash + marketable securities + receivables / current liabilities

*Interval Measure = cash + marketable securities + receivables / average daily expenditures from operations

*Cash Ratio = cash + marketable securities / current liabilities

Efficiency Ratios

*Total Asset Turnover = sales / total assets

*Average Collection Period = receivables / average daily sales

*Inventory Turnover = cost of goods sold / inventory

*Days' Sales in inventories = inventory / cost of goods sold/365

*Average Payment Period = payables / average daily expenses

Profitability Ratios

*Net Profit Margin = net income / sales

*Return on Assets = net income / assets

*Operating Profit Margin = net income + interest / sales

*Operating Return on Assets = net income + interest / total assets

*Return on Invested Capital = net income + interest / debt + preferred equity + common equity

*Return on Equity = net income / equity

*Payout Ratio = dividends / earnings

*Plowback Ratio = 1 - payout ratio

*Growth in Equity from Plowback = plowback ratio x ROE

Using Financial Ratios

Once you have selected and calculated important ratios, you still need some way of judging whether they are high or low. In essence, you need a benchmark for assessing a company's financial position. An excellent starting point is to compare them to the equivalent figures for the same company in earlier years. This will show you whether the company has improved or deteriorated in certain fundamental areas. It is also helpful to compare ratios with the ratios of competing companies in the same specific-business area as well as overall industry averages. (On a side note, don't be alarmed if you notice certain industries having very contrasting ratios with other industries. For example, the retail industry typically has a higher asset turnover and a lower operating profit margin than the steel industry. This is simply due to the nature of operating a business in this industry.

Word of Caution

Financial ratios will rarely be useful if practiced mechanically. It re□uires a large dose of good judgment. Financial ratios seldom provide answers, but they do help you ask the right questions. It is important to note that accounting data does not necessarily reflect market values correctly, and so must be used with caution. Also, accounting rules are subject to change, like everything else in life. This means that your concrete analysis may not be a fair representation of the financial position of a company after changes have been put in place, which could prove costly if you invested.

CHAPTER 2.

THE MOST CRITICAL AND KEY FINANCIALRATIOS EVERY STARTUP SHOULD KNOW

Most startups fail due to financial issues. Potential investors are keenly aware of this.

Just as the captain of a ship posts lookouts on deck for signs of danger, an entrepreneur should make use of several financial ratios to determine whether the business is about to run aground. This ratios exist to measure and judge the status ☐uo, and we review some key ratios in this document.

Through the use of these instruments, suboptimal outcomes can be foreseen, and perhaps avoided.

A Review of Assets and Liabilities

Balance sheets categorize a company's assets as either a current asset or a long-term asset. Current assets are expected to provide a benefit to the business within the next year. Long-term assets provide a benefit for more than one year.

An example of a current asset might be a certificate of deposit with a maturity of six months. A long-term asset might be a machine that is expected to operate for many years.

A company typically has several assets aside from cash on its balance sheet. The company can invest its cash in financial instruments like money market accounts, certificates of deposit, or U.S. Treasury notes. Because these investments can be converted into money rapidly, general accounting practices consider these to be cash equivalents. Cash and cash e☐uivalents are considered current assets.

Similarly, a company has current liabilities and long-term liabilities. Current liabilities are those that come due within the next year. Long-term liabilities are those that will be paid off over the course of many years.

Return on Assets

One common measure of a company is Return on Assets (ROA). Return on Assets helps the would-be investor glean insight into how profitably a business is using its assets.

If Company A shows an ROA of 9% while Company B demonstrates a 23% ROA, we see that Company B is getting much more return on its assets. The higher ROA could indicate a competitive advantage that makes Company B an attractive investment. Conversely, if you are the owner of Company A, you may do well to examine how your competition is producing more profit per dollar of assets.

The ROA formula is:

ROA = Net Income / Average Total Assets

Net income can be found readily in a company's income statement. Average total assets are calculated by adding the value of total assets at the start of the year to the value of total assets at the end of the year. Divide that sum by two.

Debt Ratio

The more debt a business assumes, the more likely the business will be unable to pay that debt. The debt ratio shows the percentage of assets that are financed with liabilities. The debt ratio formula is:

Debt Ratio = Total Liabilities / Total Assets

In spring 2017, Exxon Mobile had a debt ratio of 49% (162,989.00/330,314.00). The other 51% is financed by the stockholders of the company. By comparison, BP has a debt ratio of 64%. If an economic downturn occurs and fewer sales occur, which of these companies is more likely to default on their debts?

Current Ratio

More immediate are the current liabilities a company has: obligations that must be paid within the next year. The current ratio gives investors insight into the company's ability to pay its near-term liabilities. To do this, we employ the following formula:

Current Ratio = Total Current Assets / Total Current Liabilities

The higher the ratio, the stronger the financial state. Using the outlet hardwood flooring company Lumber Li☐uidators, we get a current ratio of 8.86. This ratio reveals that for every $1.00 of current debt Lumber Liquidators must pay off in the next year, it has $8.86 on-hand!

On the other hand, at the time of this writing, American Airlines has a current ratio of 0.76, which means the business, has only seventy-six cents for every dollar of debt it must pay off in the next year. One business clearly struggles more than the other to pay its bills.

The Acid-Test Ratio (i.e. Quick Ratio)

The acid-test ratio is a more refined version of the current ratio. The total current assets used in the current ratio are not always readily convertible into cash (should the company need to pay off debt rapidly). Significantly, inventory is excluded when using the acid-test. The formula is:

Acid-Test = Cash & Equivalents + Market. Securities + Accts. Receivable / Total Current Liabilities

When we reexamine Lumber Li□uidators with the acid-test ratio, we get a value of 0.22 - a much weaker showing than its current ratio. There are several interesting implications here. Lumber Li□uidators is a company whose current value comes primarily from its inventory. It has relatively little cash on hand. The shrewd investor can take this information and try to envision situations in which an inventory-heavy company might suffer and then estimate how likely those episodes might occur.

American Airlines, whose current assets rely less heavily on inventory and more on cash and accounts receivable, has an acid-test ratio of 0.90.

Apart from having a great product, good sales, good SEO, great marketing, and so on... there is one thing that is vital to the long term growth and success of a startup: good accounting.

Moreover, yes... you may not be as versed in numbers as your accountant is. However, do understand: it's essential to have a working knowledge of an income statement, balance sheet, and cash flow statement. Along with that a working knowledge of key financial ratios. Moreover, if these ratios are understood will make you a better entrepreneur, steward, company to buy and yes...investor. Because YOU'LL know what to look for in an upcoming company, so here are the key financial ratios every startup should:

1. Working Capital Ratio

This ratio indicates whether a company has enough assets to cover its debts.

The ratio is Current assets/Current liabilities.

(Note: current assets refer to those assets that can be turned into cash within a year, while current liabilities refers to those debts that are due within a year)

Anything below one indicates negative W/C (working capital). While anything over two means that the company is not investing excess assets; a ratio between 1.2 and 2.0 is sufficient.

So Papa Pizza, LLC has current assets are $4,615 and current liabilities are $3,003. Its current ratio would be 1.54:

($4,615/$3,003) = 1.54

2. Debt to E□uity Ratio

This is a measure of a company's total financial leverage. It's calculated by Total Liabilities/Total Assets.

(It can be applied to personal financial statements as well as corporate ones)

David's Glasses, LP has total liabilities of $100,00 and equity is $20,000 the debt to equity ratio would be 5:

($100,000/$20,000)= 5

It depends on the industry, but a ratio of 0 to 1.5 would be considered good while anything over that...not so good!

Right now David has $5 of debt for every $1 of equity...he needs to clean up his balance sheet fast!

3. Gross Profit Margin Ratio

This shows a firm's financial health to show revenue after Cost of Goods Sold (COGS) are deducted.

It is calculated as:

Revenue--COGS/Revenue=Gross Profit Margin

Let's use a bigger company as an example this time:

DEF, LLC earned $20 million in revenue while incurring $10 million in COGS related expenses, so the gross profit margin would be %50:

$20 million-$10 million/ $20 million=.5 or %50

This means for every $1 earned it has 50 cents in gross profit...not to shabby!

4. Net Profit Margin Ratio

This shows how much the company made in OVERALL profit for every $1 it generates in sales.

It's calculated as:

Net Income/Revenue=Net Profit

So Mikey's Bakery earned $97,500 in net profit on $500,000 revenue so the net profit margin is %19.5:

$97,500 net profit $500,000 revenue = 0.195 or %19.5 net profit margin

For the record: I did exclude Operating Margin as a key financial ratio. It is a great ratio as it is used to measure a company's pricing strategy and operating efficiency. However, just I excluded it does not mean you can't use it as a key financial ratio.

5. Accounts Receivable Turnover Ratio

An accounting measure used to quantify a firm's effectiveness in extending credit as well as collecting debts; also, its used to measure how efficiently a firm uses its assets.

It's calculated as:

Sales/Accounts Receivable=Receivable Turnover

So Dan's Tires earned about $321,000 in sales has $5,000 in accounts receivables, so the receivable turnover is 64.2:

$321,000/$5,000=64.2

So this means that for every dollar invested in receivables, $64.20 comes back to the company in sales.

6. Return on Investment Ratio

A performance measure used to evaluate the efficiency of an investment to compare it against other investments.

It's calculated as:

Gain from Investment-Cost of Investment/Cost of Investment=Return on Investment

So Hampton Media decides to shell out for a new marketing program. The new program cost $20,000 but is expected to bring in $70,000 in additional revenue:

$70,000-$20,000/$20,000=2.5 or 250%

So, the company is looking for a 250% return on their investment. If they get anywhere near, that...they would be happy campers:)

7. Return on E☐uity Ratio

This ratio measure's how profitable a company is with the money shareholder's have invested. Also known as "return on new worth" (RONW).

It's calculated as:

Net Income/Shareholder's E☐uity=Return on E☐uity

ABC Corp's shareholders want to see HOW well management is using capital invested. So after looking through the books for the 2009 fiscal year they see that company made $36,547 in net income with the $200,000 they invested for a return of 18%:

$36,547/$200,000= 0.1827 or 18.27%

They like what they see.

Their money's safe and is generating a pretty solid return.

Cash is the lifeblood of the business. Even when sales are good, business owners fre□uently seek out additional cash resources to grow the business - coming either from debt or e□uity. The information presented in the balance sheet, income statement, and cash flow statements are vital for external investors to decide whether to provision that money to the business. The ratios presented here provide operational insight not only for the potential investors but also for the current business owners.

SECTION 2: FINANCIAL MODELS

CHAPTER 3.

STARTUPFINANCIAL MODELS

To understand the need and importance of startup financial models, we first need to know what exactly it is that the financial sector involves itself. Financial institutions, such as investment companies, banks and security firms handle the flow of cash, the amount of which can often be of such a nature as to make it unpredictable. In some cases this amount is dependent on certain future conditions, as in e☐uity or bonds. This makes the very nature of financial transactions uncertain and unstable.

Choosing the right model

A particular context or decision should go in the actual realization of practical startup financial models. This decision or context depends on the horizon within which it has to be located. Many businesses and other financial activities re☐uire a limited horizon, while others operate within horizons that may stretch for weeks, months and maybe even years. Models that have been designed to work with continually and frequently changing data and processes would not be applicable in instances which are gradual and remain static for longer periods of time. Hence the need to choose the right type of financial model is a crucial one.

Which models are good?

While the large number of uncontrollable factors make it difficult for most startup financial models to work as focused tools for predictions. However, these models can be used for various other purposes such as risk and profit assessment, projecting the values of assumptions that are made based on existing market conditions, calculating the margins that are needed to avoid adverse situations, and various forms of sensitivity analysis. These are necessary to regulate minimum capital investment, capital allocation and measuring performance.

The best place to start a financial model from is a profound understanding of the case that requires this model. The approach is partially fulfilled by those startup financial models that contain parts of market behavior, but reality can often be vastly different from the theory that is to be followed. To understand fully the nature of all the forms of risk that the business might be exposed to, the financial model should clearly reveal the possible areas of dependencies. These dependencies can be seen between different kinds of activities and between consecutive time periods. It is also helpful if the model explains the relationship between asset types and types of business. In such a case, the way that the two sides of a balance sheet interact would be shown up clearly.

Some startup financial models

There are a number of startup financial models available for various businesses and the particular situations that they encounter. Some of the more general financial models are comparative financial analysis, cash flow forecasting and business plan models. These models look to setting up the best methods of controlling the cash that comes in and goes out. However, these are only very few of the models that are available and there are a number of business specific startup financial models in the market to choose from.

Chapter 4.

3 Tests to Ensure a Credible Financial Model for Your Start-Up

Building a good financial model is not easy but is so important to raising capital for your business. Many companies spend many hours trying to get their financial model just right. The reason - - - to provide potential investors information on the company's projected financial performance in the hopes of garnering an investment and to show that the strategy (i.e., use of dollars for such things as marketing, inventory or staffing) translate into financial gain in a reasonable period of time for that particular industry.

The model should provide the details of the big picture that the company is pitching. The key assumptions that are the drivers of the financial model are critical to understand thoroughly as well as communicate to potential investors. In addition, if you key drivers don't make sense to investors then your pitch will not be deemed credible. In order to ensure that your pitch is credible and essence your financial model makes sense, make sure to test the following items when your model has been completed BEFORE sending to anyone externally.

First Test: Make sure cash flow makes sense

In your cash flow model, you must make sure to account for when cash from sales is actually received rather than when earned and when money is paid out for expenses. Many models assume that when a sale occurs the business receives the money at the same time. However, this may be the scenario for a consumer-oriented brick and mortar retail store but not the case for an online retail store using a 3rd party sales portal to hock its products. The 3rd party may wait for 30-days or more to pay out monies for sales. In the meantime, while you are waiting for those funds, employees need to get paid and other bills are arriving in the mail. Your cash flow statement and balance sheet must take these in and outflows of cash into account. By including this information, you show potential investors that you understand cash flow and are not a complete idiot.

Second Test: You do not account for income taxes

Most models for early-stage or start-up companies show significant losses during the first years of business operations. For the years there were losses, there is no tax liability. However, when you start making a profit, there may or may not be a tax liability for the first several years depending on the earlier losses. Make sure to take into account your net operating losses from the early years when calculating future tax liabilities in the profitable years.

Taxes can be complicated so make sure to talk to a tax professional to get an understanding of your state and federal tax liabilities as well as the standard tax rate for your industry.

Third Test: Sales forecasts are based on reliable data not a percent of the market

From an investor presentation standpoint, it makes sense to present your business as garnering a certain percent of the market over a specified time period in order for the investor to understand the size of the opportunity. However, you should not build your business model on a percentage of the market assumption.

Sales should be calculated from a bottoms-up approach. This means calculating your sales based on your sales process and cycle. If you did an excellent job building out your key drivers (i.e., assumptions) of your business model, this should not be difficult to do. Examples of key drivers include:

How long does it take to close a sale?

What is the capacity per sales person to reach leads?

What is the percentage of leads that turn to sales?

What percentage of online referrals converts to paying customers?

The list can go on and on but is dependent on knowing your sales process and cycle to make it credible.

At the end of the day, it is you who is selling yourself and the company to investors. You need to understand the key drivers of your business model and explain them both strategically and financially. If you need help with the financial part, then get help. You want to be credible to potential investors.

CHAPTER 5.

THE ROLE OF FINANCIAL MODELING IN BUSINESS MODEL ANALYSIS

When a new business model is being considered, proponents must first undertake a ⬚ualitative review - i.e., determine whether the story underpinning the model makes sense. There needs to be logic behind the adoption of the model and a compelling case that it will be supported by its intended target audience.

Upon completion of the ⬚ualitative review, it is essential that a comprehensive quantitative review is then undertaken. Our experience is that far too many business owners and managers ignore this vital stage of business model assessment. Unfortunately, many believe the hard work is done once they have established a credible story about how they will make money from their proposed business or project.

For each possible business model, there is a unique set of variables - both technical and financial - which will impact upon the performance of the business. It is not enough to test movements in crucial one variable at a time. When testing new business models, it is imperative that any combination of key variables can be tested simultaneously and rapidly in order to assess the likely impact upon financial performance. This can only be achieved through the use of a customised, integrated model which has been designed for this purpose.

CHAPTER 6.

FINANCIALPROJECTIONMODELS

A crucial first step in designing an appropriate financial model for this purpose is the identification of all key drivers underpinning, and variables likely to impact upon, the financial performance of the proposed new business, business unit or project. This process is also crucial when an expansion, a merger or an ac□uisition is being contemplated. Comprehensive, sophisticated and customised financial projection models should then be designed and constructed to incorporate these drivers and variables in order to project likely financial performance across a selected period, usually five years, and to assess financial feasibility.

If done properly, these financial feasibility assessment models can become valuable management tools which can be run repeatedly in order to project financial performanceby month and year in all anticipated operating circumstances. Of particular importance, cashflow patterns can be mapped and analyzed to identify likely maximum cash re□uirements under all scenarios contemplated, thereby allowing debt and/or e□uity financing re□uirements to be planned on a timely basis.

All businesses differ in the scope and range of variables likely to impact upon financial performance. Comprehensive, well-designed and well-constructed financial models should be able to easily and repeatedly test for the effects of changes in all variables likely to impact upon the financial performance of the business, project or investee entity. Importantly, they should also be able to test all relevant permutations and combinations of relevant variable sets, and to estimate the effects of both upside and downside departures from the anticipated scenario.

Bridging the Gap between Financial Modeling and Budgeting

A financial model and an operating budget are two different things, but the two should correlate with and complement each other. I'm going to briefly discuss the differences, what each is used for, and how to use them both more effectively to run and improve your business.

THE DIFFERENCES

Financial modeling/forecasting usually takes a big-picture approach and avoids too many details. The model is used to assess opportunities and the cause and effect of major business decisions. The model is often expressed in terms of yearly performance.

An operating budget, in contrast, is mired in the details. It needs to tie directly to the accounting system's general ledger or chart of accounts for QuickBooks users, and is usually a month-by-month forecast of the activities of each account for the next 12 to 24 months. Use of the operating budget includes analysis of the budget vs. actual performance each month.

HOW & WHY SHOULD THEY CORRELATE?

A business needs to have both a financial model and an operating budget. A budget without a long-term model/forecast leaves a company pretty directionless and lacking the ability to understand the impact of business decisions on financial performance. A financial model without an operating budget is like a "pie-in-the-sky" dream that can't be founded in reality. There is no way to track progress towards accomplishing the goals and objectives, if they are even outlined, and it is almost impossible to hold anyone accountable. Every business should have both.

The place where many companies go wrong is that they do not actively both of them and ensure they "feed" into one another. For example, let's assume we have modeled $5,000,000 in sales for 2009 but our operating budget calls for $3,500,000. This discrepancy is large and invalidates one, the other, or both!

The operating budget needs to validate and complement the assumptions made in the financial model, and vice-versa. In fact, the monthly review of the budget vs. actual performance can often generate valuable information about our assumptions and can justify changes and updates regularly to the financial model.

For example, let's assume we project a 50% gross profit in our 5-year financial model. Due to changes in the economy, increasing material prices, and a slight change in mix of products, our gross profit is coming in every month at 45%. We find and track this in our operating budget analysis each month. Since the trend seems to be consistent, we may make a decision to update the gross profit assumption in our financial model.

Most emerging companies may not have the expertise to generate and use these tools to their benefit. By finding a professional that offers CFO services, most businesses can maximize the benefit of these tools at a very affordable cost.

With an understanding of the differences between a financial model and budget, we can see the need to bridge the gap between the long-term planning and short-term budgeting so that they complement each other. While this requires some effort and expertise, the result is always a competitive advantage in terms of a more effective execution of our business model. That means more cash flow and better profitability that your competitors, which results in a sustainable competitive advantage.

CHAPTER 7.

A FINANCIAL MODEL THAT DRIVES YOUR SUCCESS

"Creating a solid financial model and using it to run your business is one of the fundamental actions required to build a successful business" (Lance Weatherby Blog, 18 Oct 2007). Assembling the dynamic and fixed parts of the financial structure of a business creates a powerful tool - a financial model. However, failing to use it to run and improve your business renders it powerless. We hope to briefly discuss some of the benefits that may come if you discipline yourself to participate in and regularly revisit this exercise.

WHY CREATE THE MODEL

Here are the words of a budding entrepreneur: "I had a mentor who sat me down and built a financial model for me. He asked me, 'How many days does it take to do this? How many people does it take to do that?' Building on the answers to those and many other □uestions, he was able to predict the company's future several years down the lines, a big plus in meeting with venture capitalists" ("Speaking From Experience," Entrepreneur.com, 11 Jan 2008). Your model can help you see years into the future and help you appropriately capitalize your business.

FORECASTING THE FUTURE

Business owners often see no value in trying to understand the future because, as they might say, "I do not know what's going to happen in the future." While their statement is probably right, it fails to consider that forecasting the future empowers them to make the best decisions as the future becomes the present.

Here is an example from a real company doing about $10 million in annual sales. The company saw a decrease in its sales in 2007 of 21%. The firm's financial model helped the owners maneuver through its unforeseen internal and external challenges, tweak part of their revenue and cost structure, and still have a very profitable year. More importantly, the firm will, as a result of its corrections in 2007, increase sales in 2008 by at least 44% and reach an entirely new level of profitability. Without their financial model as a guide, they would have lost money in 2007 and would be struggling to return to a break-even status in 2008.

VIABILITY AND CREDIBILITY

You will struggle to receive debt and/or e□uity financing if you do not have a firm grasp of your financial model. Lenders, angel investors, venture capitalists, and often friends and family want to see the financial model and understand how it works. They will ask questions about your assumptions and may want to look at your historical performance to validate your claims. Your model will also clarify the amount of external money required, your intended use of the funds, and the repayment period or return on investment your financier can expect.

CHAPTER 8.

BUILDING A FINANCIAL MODEL

A lot of investors rely on analysts' forecasts when they are assessing the potential value of a stock. That's not necessarily a bad idea; analysts have privileged access to companies' directors and often have substantial experience and expertise in their sector.

Still, if you really want to do your own research, you're going to need to start building your own financial models. For some stocks, there aren't any forecasts available; for others, the single forecast out there might be out of date, or it's a forecast by the broker, which you can expect to be somewhat optimistic in many cases.

Besides, even if there are other forecasts out there, building your own model will give you an in-depth understanding of the company and its business, far more than just reading the annual report.

First, you'll need to assess the business model of the company. Is there a convenient unit of volume? For instance, it is houses with house builders, kilowatt hours with electricity companies, and so on. That might apply on the cost side too; for retailers, square meter of retail space is an important figure. Given these units, you will often be able to estimates revenues and at least some of the costs - this is extremely useful, as you can then analyse where growth is coming on - is it coming from the increased volume of sales, or just increased prices?

You will also need to look at whether gross margin or operating margin is the key ratio. For retailers, it's gross margin - effectively that measures what mark-up they're making on their goods. For a software company, on the other hand, the gross margin is usually 90% of more - there's practically no cost of sales - so its operating margin that is more important.

If a company has mainly staff costs, you can estimate the number of staff and what they're likely to be paid - obviously a caterer or construction company will tend to have lower costs per employee than a computer consultancy or investment manager.

Start off with the last couple of years' real figures, and then simply build up next year in the same format. By employing unit-based forecasts, or by looking at what margin you might expect, and using a chosen growth rate for revenue, you can build up next year's profit and loss account. For instance, with a computing firm I might look at what other firms in its area are making as operating profit margins - and then forecast, say, it will have margins a couple of percent lower, because it has some duplication of costs while it's setting up an Indian outsourcing arm.

You might also adjust the margins if you know that cost inputs are increasing - for instance, in the food industry or in brewing, where malt and hops shot up in price in 2008-9.

Once you've created the model, you need to check it. A good way to do this is to work out the other ratios - for instance you might work out contractor day rates for a computer company by working out the daily cost per employee, and doubling it. That's very rule of thumb but it should give you an idea of whether the model is working.

A huge advantage of having this kind of model is that you can flex it. You can say 'what if' the price of fuel went up again? What impact would it have on British Airways? You can ask 'what if' a company hired more staff, 'what if' Marston's closed a few pubs, 'what if' the rate of bad debt at Lloyds increased.

Broker forecasts all make assumptions, and you do not really know what those assumptions are - you can make a range, and you will be picking assumptions that you think are viable. If you are a contrarian investor, you may end up with a rather different result from many of the analysts, simply because you have made different assumptions about the economy, or the oil price.

Moreover, when the results of the company report, you will be able to check your model - and your assumptions. You can really hold the company to account, because you have a financial model that will show you precisely what is going on.

SECTION 3: BUSINESS VALUATION

CHAPTER 9.

REASONS TO PERFORM A BUSINESS VALUATION

Why a Business Valuation?

Many business owners, business buyers, business sellers and others need business valuations for a wide range of purposes. Those purposes range from considering the sale or purchase of a business to complying with a court order to settle a legal issue. Often, business owners just want to have an idea of the current value of their business.

Here are some of the reasons people come to us or use our business valuation software tool for business valuation.

Curiosity

Just as people like to check their stock portfolio from time to time, small business owners like to get an idea of their company's value and changes in its value. Our valuation tool can give you a good idea of your business' value, based upon your answers to several financial and non-financial questions. A basic valuation is free!

Buying a Business, Initial Evaluation

Often, business buyers are bewildered as to how a seller arrives at an asking price for his or her business. In some cases, the asking price is not based on any rhyme or reason. Before getting too involved in negotiating a business acquisition, it is a good idea to determine if the asking price is in the ballpark. A difference of 10% to 25% (asking price vs. independent valuation) is usually bridgeable. However, if the difference is much more than 25% or so, chances of buyer and seller getting to an agreement are pretty slim.

Buying a Business, Offer & Negotiation Phase

Once it's determined that buyer and seller are in the same ballpark, a more formal valuation will be very helpful. It's one thing to ask a seller to lower his price by 20%; It's quite another to show that seller an independent valuation that details the reasons for your offer price.

Selling a Business, Early Preparation

The decision to sell a business rarely happens overnight, and neither should the planning. The time to start planning for the sale of a business is 1 to 3 years prior to the target date of the sale. A key element of the planning is an objective opinion your company's value. This is important not only for setting reasonable expectations and a reasonable asking price. It's also important because there are some clear step you can take to enhance the value of your company, and to make the sale easier and quicker if you start the planning in advance.

Selling a Business within One Year

If you are planning to offer your business for sale within a year, it's definitely time to get a valuation along with a little professional guidance. Setting the wrong asking price or even the right asking price without documentation to support it can be deadly. Also, there is a lot you can and should do to make the business more salable (and more valuable) if you do not wait until it is too late.

Taking on a New Partner or Buying Out a Current Partner

Note that in this context we are using partner to mean any person or entity that has ownership. It can be a stockholder in a corporation, a member of an LLC, or a partner in the legal sense; a partner in a partnership entity.

More often than not there is a difference of opinion as to the value of one's partnership (or stock or membership share) in a closely held company. A third party valuation is the best way to mitigate disagreements and arrive at a fair buyout (or buy-in) deal.

Loan Proposal

Banks and other lenders use a number of different criteria in making lending decisions. A good independent business valuation can make the difference between a loan rejection and an approval. In the current tight lending environment, a business borrower needs every advantage he can muster to get that approval.

Loan Proposal, SBA

The Small Business Administration (SBA) has specific rules for business valuations that it will accept (as detailed in SBA SOP 50-10 5b). If you are applying for a SBA direct or SBA guaranteed loan, it is important that any submitted valuation adhere to SBA rules.

Raising Venture Capital or Independent Investment

Professional venture capitalists as well as independent investors are first and foremost looking for a return on their investment. While investors understand that they are taking a risk, a well-documented independent valuation can go a long way toward mitigating the perceived risk, and toward getting you the right deal for the investment you need.

Estate Planning

For many business owners, the largest single element of their estate is the business they own. However, many business owners in this circumstance don't know the value of their largest holding. For a myriad of reasons ranging from tax planning to assure your wishes are accurately carried out without difficulty or conflict, a business valuation is essential for proper estate planning.

Estate Settlement

When a going business is an asset of an estate, a valuation is essential and often required by a court, taxing authority, or both. Unfortunately, disagreements are common in lots of aspects of estate settlement, and the value of a business that's in the estate is no exception. It is not uncommon that contesting parties will each retain valuation experts who ascribe significantly different values to the same business. It is best to hire a valuation expert who has extensive experience with valuations for estate purposes and in testifying to defend his or her valuation in court.

Divorce and other Legal Purposes

Business valuations are very often needed for divorce settlements and other settlements where a court or arbitrator is called upon to make decisions regarding fairness. In these situations, it is not uncommon that contesting parties will each retain valuation experts who ascribe significantly different values to the same business. In a situation that may end up in front of a judge or arbitrator, it is best to hire a valuation expert who has experience in courtroom testimony.

Enhance the Value of a Business

There are relatively easy steps that can enhance the value and salability of many if not most businesses. This involves analyzing the business' weakness from a buy-sell perspective and correcting those weaknesses. Some steps for example are as easy as putting verbal agreements into writing or securing a lease renewal option. Other steps take a bit more effort but can be well worth that effort. The place to start is with an initial valuation that identifies a company's strengths and weaknesses and the estimated cost, effort, and benefit to mitigate those weaknesses. We would be happy to discuss the possibilities of enhancing your company's value and salability, prior to putting it on the market.

CHAPTER 10.

BUSINESS VALUATION - EVERYTHING A BUSINESS OWNERSHOULDKNOW

The motive to find the value of a business might range from buying/selling business decisions, raising capital through borrowings, planning strategic mergers and acquisition plans etc.

The below article throws light on some of the major issues faced during business valuation and tips on how to deal with such issues.

Issue 1: How to select the right business evaluator?

Ask this simple question "Am I qualified and experienced to evaluate my own business?"

If it is an unchartered territory seek business professionals listed below who usually offers such services:

1. CPAs offer business valuation services. The knowledge gained from handling various accounting, finance and tax work allows an experienced CPA to gain knowledge that is well suited for valuing a business

2. Financial experts/consultants (Non-CPA) can also lend their expertise, but their background and experience need to be investigated carefully before hiring them.

3. Business Brokers are an obvious choice to value the businesses for sale as they have many years specialization in buying business and selling business which involves business valuation

4. Commercial Real Estate Brokers/Agents are good at appraising real estate, but lack skills and experience to properly value intangible assets like goodwill.

Issue 2: What are the most commonly followed business valuation techniques?

There are many methods to find the value of business but the most popular methods adopted by professional and experienced business brokers are the following:

Letter of Opinion:

The Letter of Opinion is a restricted use valuation intended for small companies with sales less than $250,000. The basis of this valuation is a market comparison with like companies within an industry.

Value Analysis:

The Value Analysis is a discretionary cash flow since most Main Street businesses are bought and sold on a multiple of annual cash flow.

Formal Business Valuation:

It involves financial analysis, review of the Balance sheet with support documents containing reviews of companies historical and project earnings.

M&A Valuation:

The Mergers and Acquisitions Valuation is a comprehensive business valuation for transactional purposes and is developed in accordance with the Uniform Standards of Professional Appraisal Practice (USPAP).

IRS Revenue Ruling 59-60:

A USPAP governed valuation developed for litigation focusing on US Court Reviews, Cited Court Precedents, and in-depth analysis and research of minority and marketability discounts.

Issue 3: What are the preparatory information and documents required for business valuation?

Following is a checklist of documents and information that professional business advisors ask prior business valuation:

Financial Statements:

These includes balance sheets, income statements, statement of changes in financial position, stockholder's equity or partner's capital holdings statements for last 5 fiscal years, list of subsidiaries, list of equipment's, depreciation schedule, aged accounts receivable or payment, prepaid expenses, inventory list, leases (if any), existing contracts with employees, suppliers, franchise agreements, customer agreements, royalty agreements, equipment lease or rentals, loan agreements, labor contract, employee benefit plan, compensation schedule for owners, insurances in force, budgets of projects, if available.

Company Documents:

These includes, articles of incorporation (if any), by-laws, any amendments to either, corporate minutes, partnerships, articles of partnerships (with any amendments) along with list of existing buy/sell agreements, options to purchase stock or partnership interest, or rights of first refusal.

Other Information:

Also keeps ready details of company history, changes in ownership and /or bona-fide offers received. Also describe the position as compared to competitors or any other factor making the business unique, relevant marketing literature like brochures, advertisements, list of location where company operates, details in terms of size, and whether it is fully owned or leased. List of states in which the company is licensed to do business, list of current customers, suppliers, major accounts. Resumes of, or list of, key personnel, with age, position, compensation, length of service, education and prior experience. List of memberships with Trade associations or would be eligible for membership. List of any patent, copyright, trademark, and other intangible asset along with correspondence with regulatory agencies for issues related to business.

Issue 4: How is the business valuation undertaken?

Adopting a right business valuation process ensures the sale of business will bring in a better sale price compared to arbitrary valuation of business.

Step 1: The Broker meets with the client to determine what type of valuation is required.

Step 2: During the meeting, the Broker will assist in the completion of the Company Profile information needed for the type of valuation selected.

Step 3: Once the Company Profile has been completed the package of information is mailed, faxed, or emailed to third party Valuation Analyst.

Step 4: The Valuation Analyst will review the documents and begin the valuation.

Step 5: A completed Company Profile is then generated, and all questions that arise are answered.

Step 6: The Analyst will issue a preliminary review of the valuation. It assures that all details have been considered and allows for any adjustments based on new information or further clarifications.

Step 7: Once the review with the business broker has been conducted, the Analyst will finalize, print, and send the final valuation report.

Step 8: The Broker will receive hard copies and an electronic copy (if requested) of the final report. This report is sent to the business seller/owner.

A planned business valuation involves lot of procedures and systematic planning to ensure the right value is found out to help sell business.

Business Valuation: Estimate Worth of Your Business

There are some occasions when business owners want to know or estimate the worth of their business. It is very imperative to assess business valuation to get to know that whether you have significant asset or liability. Mostly, true valuation of business occurs only when business owners sell the business. However, there are four basic methods of business valuation such as Asset Based valuation, Earnings Based, Market based, and Cash-Flow based. There is a common step which comes under all the methods, compilation of relevant and accurate financial information of the company.

In simple language, business valuation is a set of simple steps used to determine the value of the business or market value of the organization.

Asset approach - This approach is used to determine the liquidation worth of an operating business. It is a very effective approach to estimate the replacement value or liuidation value of the business.

Market based approach - In this approach, valuation of your business will depend on the analysis of different similar business to get estimate value or company valuation.

Earning Based Approach - It is closely integrated with the market approach. There is a categorized formula to determine the earning based company valuation.

Valuation = Average of normal EBT/capitalization rate

Cash Flow Based valuation - This approach is just similar to the earning based approach. It estimates the value of business depending on the future coming cash into the business.

All these methods can be applied to estimate company valuation in the market. Sometimes, reasons of estimating valuations might be just to sell off the company. Whatsoever the reasons are, you just need to consider the factors that influence company valuation process and methods precisely. Here are some factors that can affect the process of valuation.

* Company's overall performance and condition

* Reason for selling or estimating the value

* Competition - moderate, limited and severe

* Legal rules and regulations

* Selection of method and procedures

* Business assets

Business valuation is a combination of art and science, which focus on the current value or worth of the business after analyzing other related factors. It is a complete educated guess to provide worth of the company or business to the owners for several purposes whether for selling or only determining the asset and liability. There are several websites who offer services of expert and experienced person to judge and evaluate the value of companies and business in the market.

CHAPTER 11.

BUSINESS VALUATION FAQS

Considered a part of the annual strategic planning process, business valuation is the process of determining the estimated market value of a business enterprise. It is a valuable tool for business owners, stockowners and investors. Business valuation is used for a variety of purposes such as buy/sell agreements, mergers and acquisitions, estate planning, bankruptcies and pension plans.

1. Why is business valuation important?

Business valuation is very important as it is regarded as the heart of a buy-sell agreement instituted between business owners. It is important not only for a business owner preparing for a sale but also for numerous business and legal situations that need a detailed valuation.

Business valuation is conducted while buying or selling shares to employees, planning gifts to heirs, retiring and selling to other family members, providing ade␣uate key man insurance coverage and creating a basis for compensating key non-family management.

2. What is the different business valuation methods?

There are several methods to determine the market value of an enterprise. Business valuation methods are categorized as market-based methods, income-based methods, asset-based methods and hybrid methods. One can select the method depending on the particular valuation need.

3. What are the reasons for conducting a business valuation?

Business valuation is conducted for the valuation for tax purposes and ownership transfer. Besides, it is necessary for financing or insurance purposes.

4. What is the factors to be considered in a business valuation process?

Business earnings, availability of assets, nature of the business, and history of the enterprise from its inception, the enterprise's goodwill and other intangible values, economic outlook in general, outlook of the specific industry, book value of the stock, and the financial condition of the business are some of the factors to be considered during a business valuation process.

5. How much do business valuation services cost?

The cost of business valuation services varies significantly with the size and complexity of the business being evaluated. Other factors such as business cash flow, age of business, owner involvement, revenue, availability of vendor financing and profitability also determine the costs. In general, the cost of business valuation services range from a minimum of $1500 to thousands of dollars.

OTHER BOOKS BY (ANDREI BESEDIN)

1) **50 MOST POWERFUL EXCEL FUNCTIONS AND FORMULAS: ADVANCED WAYS TO SAVE YOUR TIME AND MAKE COMPLEX ANALYSIS QUICK AND EASY!**
HTTPS://WWW.AMAZON.COM/MOST-POWERFUL-EXCEL-FUNCTIONS-FORMULAS/DP/1521549915/REF=ZG_BS_132559011_7?_ENCODING=UTF8&PSC=1&REFRID=QT5D1NR6CBRAFTGEP7AG

2) **SECRETS OF LOOKUP: BECOME MORE PRODUCTIVE WITH VLOOKUP, FREE YOUR TIME!** HTTPS://WWW.AMAZON.COM/SECRETS-LOOKUP-PRODUCTIVE-VLOOKUP-TRAINING-EBOOK/DP/B073P4FVSG/REF=LA_B07211P1NS_1_10?S=BOOKS&IE=UTF8&QID=1499524730&SR=1-10

3) **TOP 3 EXCEL FORMULAS AND FUNCTIONS** HTTPS://WWW.AMAZON.COM/EXCEL-FORMULAS-FUNCTIONS-TRAINING-BOOK-EBOOK/DP/B0738LF8LL/REF=SR_1_6?IE=UTF8&QID=1499524945&SR=8-6&KEYWORDS=TOP+3+EXCEL

4) **AMAZING JAVA: LEARN JAVA QUICKLY!**
https://www.amazon.com/Amazing-JAVA-Learn-Quickly-ebook/dp/B0737762M8/ref=la_B07211P1NS_1_2?s=books&ie=UTF8&qid=1499524891&sr=1-2&refinements=p_82%3AB07211P1NS

5) **DASH DIET TO MAKE MIDDLE AGED PEOPLE HEALTHY AND FIT: 40 DELICIOUS RECIPES FOR PEOPLE OVER 40 YEARS OLD!**
https://www.amazon.com/Dash-Diet-Middle-People-Healthy-ebook/dp/B071WZBZPB/ref=la_B07211P1NS_1_3?s=books&ie=UTF8&qid=1499524891&sr=1-3&refinements=p_82%3AB07211P1NS

6) **MEDITERRANEAN DIET FOR MIDDLE AGED PEOPLE: 40 DELICIOUS RECIPES TO MAKE PEOPLE OVER 40 YEARS OLD HEALTHY AND FIT!**
https://www.amazon.com/Mediterranean-diet-middle-aged-people-ebook/dp/B0723952FH/ref=la_B07211P1NS_1_4?s=books&ie=UTF8&qid=1499524891&sr=1-4&refinements=p_82%3AB07211P1NS

7) **FITNESS FOR MIDDLE AGED PEOPLE: 40 POWERFUL EXERCISES TO MAKE PEOPLE OVER 40 YEARS OLD HEALTHY AND FIT!**
https://www.amazon.com/Fitness-Middle-Aged-People-Exercises-ebook/dp/B072VFBT99/ref=la_B07211P1NS_1_5?s=books&ie=UTF8&qid=1499524891&sr=1-5&refinements=p_82%3AB07211P1NS

8) **MARKET RESEARCH: GLOBAL MARKET FOR GERMANIUM AND GERMANIUM PRODUCTS**
https://www.amazon.com/Market-Research-Global-Germanium-Products-ebook/dp/B00X4JBM92/ref=la_B07211P1NS_1_9?s=books&ie=UTF8&qid=1499524891&sr=1-9&refinements=p_82%3AB07211P1NS

9) **STOCKS, MUTUAL FUNDS:THE START UP GUIDE ON STOCK INVESTING**

https://www.amazon.com/Stocks-Mutual-Funds-Start-Investing-ebook/dp/B00WOGXCDU/ref=la_B07211P1NS_1_6?s=books&ie=UTF8&qid=1499524891&sr=1-6&refinements=p_82%3AB07211P1NS

10) Aerobics, running & jogging: 30 Minutes a Day Burn Fat Workout for Middle Aged Men"!: Two most powerful ways to burn fat quickly!

https://www.amazon.com/Aerobics-running-jogging-Minutes-powerful-ebook/dp/B00WA9ESG6/ref=la_B07211P1NS_1_7?s=books&ie=UTF8&qid=1499524891&sr=1-7&refinements=p_82%3AB07211P1NS

11) Diamond Cut Six Packs: How To Develop Fantastic Abs
https://www.amazon.com/Diamond-Cut-Six-Packs-Fantastic-ebook/dp/B01E2OELVS/ref=la_B07211P1NS_1_8?s=books&ie=UTF8&qid=1499524891&sr=1-8&refinements=p_82%3AB07211P1NS

12) 15 MOST POWERFUL FEATURES OF PIVOT TABLES!: Save Your Time With MS Excel!
https://www.amazon.com/MOST-POWERFUL-FEATURES-PIVOT-TABLES-ebook/dp/B074THF418/ref=sr_1_3?ie=UTF8&qid=1504594835&sr=8-3&keywords=besedin

13) 20 Most Powerful Excel Conditional Formatting Techniques!: Save Your Time With MS Excel
https://www.amazon.com/Powerful-Excel-Conditional-Formatting-Techniques-ebook/dp/B074H9W6XJ/ref=sr_1_4?ie=UTF8&qid=1504594835&sr=8-4&keywords=besedin

14) Secrets of MS Excel VBA/Macros for Beginners: Save Your Time With Visual Basic Macros!
https://www.amazon.com/Secrets-Excel-VBA-Macros-Beginners-ebook/dp/B075GYBLWT/ref=sr_1_7?ie=UTF8&qid=1506057725&sr=8-7&keywords=besedin

15) Secrets of Business Plan Writing: Business Plan Template and Financial Model Included!

https://www.amazon.com/Secrets-Business-Plan-Writing-Financial-ebook/dp/B076GJK8T1/ref=sr_1_9?ie=UTF8&qid=1509858352&sr=8-9&keywords=besedin

16) Secrets of Access Database Development and Programming!

https://www.amazon.com/Secrets-Access-Database-Development-Programming-ebook/dp/B0776FZVG6/ref=sr_1_6?s=books&ie=UTF8&qid=1510391273&sr=1-6&keywords=besedin

THANK YOU BUT CAN I ASK YOU FOR A FAVOR?

Let me say thank you for downloading and reading my book. This would be all about the secrets of financial analysis and modeling. Hope you enjoyed it but you need to keep on learning to be perfect!If you enjoyed this book, found it useful or otherwise then I'd really grateful it if you would post a short review on Amazon. I read all the reviews personally so I can get your feedback and make this book even better.

Thanks for your support!

29320690R00031

Printed in Poland
by Amazon Fulfillment™
Poland Sp. z o.o., Wrocław